the little book of moments

Jeff Chandler

ISBN: 978-1-48407-153-3

DEDICATION

For Alex Jnr. – The little man with a big heart.

CONTENTS

ACKNOWLEDGMENTS

When I started my blog (malleablereality.com) three years ago, I had no idea that it would be the start of a journey that would change my life forever.

Love goes out to my beautiful family who are the constant connection to my past, present and future.

To each and every one of my amazing friends who have been there through thick and thin, always with an open heart and a wise word or two, I will never be able to thank you enough.

The love and support I have received from my family of blog followers in this time has left me awe-inspired, and given me a renewed sense of hope for our crazy, beautiful blue planet. To each and every one, I thank you from the bottom of my heart!

Finally, to Sean…Thank you for giving this book the most beautifully drawn illustrations! It wouldn't be the same without you, and your unconditional love and never-ending support is the reason for who I am today.

PROLOGUE

I knew it was going to be one of those days right from the start...

Already running late, I sped out the door and made my way hurriedly down the stairs to come out onto the street.

And that's when I tripped.

Flying through the air, there was no time to react as my entire body catapulted forwards. The surroundings morphed into a blur with nothing but cool morning air rushing past. And so I found myself lying flat on my face, cold pavement pressed up against my cheek. Great!

I stared up at the darkening rain clouds and sighed deeply before picking myself up, dusting myself down, and continuing onwards. I quickened my pace before the impending downpour; suits, bags, umbrellas, and shoes, all weaving in and out of each other like a hypnotic dance around me.

And then the second slap of the day arrived.

No sooner had I turned the corner than I was buffeted by a freak gust of wind, which must have travelled all the way across London to greet me with an eyeful of swirling dust. Rubbing furiously at my tightly closed eyes must have been a cue for the heavens to open. And so, with my umbrella up, I watched helplessly as it flipped inside out and was soaked in less than a minute. This was turning into quite a day!

Standing on a packed Central line platform, I watched as train after crowded train came and went in a metropolitan blur; strangers' faces squashed against every last piece of steel and glass.

With a whoosh of warm air, the headlights snaked out of the tunnel and the train decelerated noisily into the station.

Enter stage left: the man who thought he owned the world.

Now, I've always believed in the value of good manners and the importance of respect, so when I found myself being forcibly pushed sideways out of the way, I was shocked...and slightly angry. Being a mere 5'6, this 6ft something giant brushed me aside with the greatest of ease. Suddenly swept along with the rest of the people behind me, I landed in the carriage with nowhere else to go. Doors tightly closed, we lurched forwards and sped off into the darkness. Once inside the tunnel, the unfriendly giant began to shuffle around, not actually caring in the slightest that his oversized newspaper was being supported by my smothered face.

"Excuse me!" (muffling through crumpled print)

"What?!" (sneering)

"Well, let me think…first you shove me out of the way in order to get on the train before everyone else, and then you move around with no concern for anyone but yourself - there are other people on this planet, you know!" (frustrated).

After many heated words and a sprinkling of pushing and shoving in our semi-embraced entanglement, I decided to end our relationship with the words "You are a very rude man!", and that was that - silence rang throughout the carriage, leaving nothing but the sound of dripping umbrellas and papers turning to echo off the walls.

Walking up the escalators and out onto the bustling street, I took a deep breath. Why did life seem so difficult, so challenging lately? Every day was like a struggle at the moment and there didn't seem to be a great deal of joy any more. Thoughts rushed through my head at the speed of light, searching inside for elusive answers to how I could get out of this rut - this rut which seemed to be dragging me down. Then, as cool autumn rain ran down my back, something caught my eye - something bright and yellow on the floor. At first I couldn't make out what it was...and then it came into focus. Lying on its own in the middle of the glistening grey pavement was a single carnation flower. Where it came from I had no idea, but there was something about seeing it here that made my spirit lift. It seemed strangely out of place and it was just enough to make me open my eyes just that little bit wider. Instantly, I felt the pressures of the morning wash slowly away as a smile crept across my cold, wet face. Then it hit me - I had become so wrapped up in the difficulties that life presented on a daily basis, that I was actually oblivious to so much - all the special little things that go unnoticed right under my very nose.

There and then I decided to look at life in a different way. Whenever possible, I would pay close attention to every detail and be present in the moment. If I could stop for just a few seconds to notice a flower on the floor and instantly feel better, what else could I begin to notice?

Over the following weeks I became the observer - looking around to see the things outside of myself, things that I had missed before and capturing them like scenes in a movie, I started to see the warm smile

3

from a stranger, the door being held open for me and the birdsong that swam in the air...

I've noticed that something wonderful happens when we open up: our breathing becomes deeper, we stand taller, feel lighter, and our tense muscles begin to loosen up.

As an experiment, right now, stop reading this and close your eyes for a minute. Notice everything around you - what can you hear and smell? Is your forehead scrunched up or loose? Is your posture hunched over or lifted tall? And your breathing - is it shallow and quick or deep and slow? Once we take notice of these basic elements, we begin to expand. Stress leaves our body, and for a short while, we are present, living in the moment.

And that is where happiness lies - not in the past or even in the future, but right here and right now.

I've read my fair share of self-help books, and as beautifully uplifting as they were, the concepts held within the pages seemed somewhat abstract to me. I always seem to feel changed for a short while before sinking back into my usual routine once again.

And so, I wanted to write something simple - the simplest path to happiness I had discovered that could be used as a basis for everything we do in life. Through my own personal experiences, I want to share with you my special moments and the lessons that I have learnt along the way.

There's absolutely nothing extraordinary about this process and it certainly isn't difficult to master...but it works beautifully to lift mind, body and spirit.

Taking a sideways look at life, love and everything in between, the bite-sized snapshots within this book will lift and inspire you. You can dip into them any time you like, whether travelling to work or last thing at night before going to sleep.

And so, with an outstretched hand, I invite you to come with me on my journey through the ordinary to uncover the magic that surrounds us.

After all, it's not what you look at that matters...it's what you see.

EVERYTHING

As I lie on my back with the warm grass tickling my skin, I look up. The sky is crystal blue and the dazzling rays twinkle through the swaying branches overhead. A plane full of people draws a white line 37,000ft above and disappears behind the trees. I close my eyes and feel everything around me: the slight breeze on my arms, the warmth on my face, the money spider struggling to make its way across my hairy leg. I love these moments where I can shut out the world and just be. Life is so full of 'stuff' that we sometimes get lost in it, like my eight-legged friend now weaving in and out.

I watch the family walking past and wonder if one day, in years to come, the little girl will lie on the grass, look up, and remember that beautiful sunny morning she took her mum and dad to the park.

My reverie is abruptly shattered by the sound of a screaming girlfriend being pushed into the lido pool, followed by a big splash and louder laughter from the pair. I smile as a bee buzzes past my nose making me

move my head to the side.
Everything is perfect, and for the briefest of
moments, I have everything I will ever need.
Life is beautiful.

IL BEL VIAGGIO

I once whizzed through the streets of Florence on the back of a bike...

Squeezing the helmet onto my head, I felt the foam cover my ears and turn the bustle of the city down to a muffle. Once I was settled in my seat, my friend turned around to look at me.

"Ready?", he asked with a cheeky grin.

With a nod from me, we were off. I was amazed at how quickly we accelerated over the cobbled street and out into the open. I'm sure I felt my hair blowing in the wind under the helmet. The rush literally took my breath away.

With every twist and turn I had to remind myself to hold on for dear life and stay seated. Cars came and went in a Florentine blur. After a while I felt my body relax as I started to breathe. It was amazing and exhilarating and freeing. The city looked stunning at this velocity.

And on we rode. I never once stopped smiling.

"How was that?", he asked pulling off his helmet.

"Incredible!", I declared with a massive grin.

Stepping off, he laughed and confided that because I had held on so tightly to the bike it was harder for him to ride, and actually changed the way we handled the road. He could feel every bit of tension in my body through the bike. As we continued to laugh, I suddenly realised something: Life will always have its hairy moments, and sometimes, we just have to let go and move with the flow - the tighter we hold on, the more difficult the ride.

The beautiful streets of Florence whispered in my ear that evening. She told me to be light with life and everything will always be ok.

APRIL SHOWERS

As the darkening clouds churn above and quickly
expand, I know what is coming.
Feeling the gusty wind pick up to send the white
blossom dancing around me like confetti, all the hairs
on my body stand up to greet the change. That
familiar scent hangs in the air: a mixture of damp
woodland foliage and floral cardboard. Remembering
how the sun had tenderly stroked my hair this
afternoon, I quicken my pace along the tree-lined
street towards home.
I start to think about our beautiful season that has
returned once again with a pile of delicately wrapped
gifts stashed under her arms and a little surprise. I
have missed this old friend.
Spring always fills me with optimism and hope - a
breath of fresh air to carry us along our journey. It is
the season to forgive and forget, to let go and grow.
I smile as I close my eyes, feeling the first few drops
of cool spring rain splash onto my face and run down
my neck. The heavens open and in less than three

seconds I am soaked through, but it doesn't matter one bit. Spring is back!

BREAKFAST WITH A FRIEND

As my eyes slowly opened to see the early morning sun peeking through a gap in the curtains, I was aware of a strange tip-tapping at the window. Stumbling sleepily across the room, I pulled back the curtain to find, staring up at me, a beautiful mallard duck. With eyes locked, our curiosity over each other held us fixated. I couldn't help but smile broadly as I stared at my new friend who had wandered over to look for me whilst I was sleeping just minutes earlier. Looking into his beautifully cheeky eyes I started to think about all the things that make up his being and what I admire most about him. His feathers are perfectly waterproofed, allowing any unwanted and hurtful stuff to flow away literally like water off a duck's back. His ability to take off almost vertically to clear any obstacle is an inspiration to anyone who believes that it is too challenging to soar in the face of adversity. Once in flight, my friend can reach speeds of up to 70ft per second because he believes it is possible. He also does an awesome job of looking cool and composed as he works hard to move forward in the current-filled water.

I decided it was time for breakfast and we bonded over a loaf of bread which was well received by both of us. After our feast, he tilted his head and stared at me for a moment. We both froze with hearts wide open. Everything stopped.

Then with one last tip of his head I watched as he turned, quacked, and waddled away back into the forest from whence he came.

I laughed and wished him a long and happy life.

THE SECOND GUESS

Pick a number, any number and I will tell you what
you are thinking...
It can come from a missing text or a silent stare, a
status update or a shift in body language. A million
questions are sent flying through our synapses faster
than the speed of light, all to fill in the missing gaps.
What does this mean? What are they thinking? Is it
anything or everything to do with me? At the slightest
whiff of doubt or missing information, we jump into
action and set our minds to work. Racing through a
million and one possibilities, we finally come to rest at
the one which seems most logical, unaware that we
could be facing in totally the wrong direction.
I am sure I'm not the only one who has ever put 2
and 2 together to come up with E=MC2 to the power
of wrong. Who knew that being a mind reader would
be so exhausting!
We are all so complex and unique that it is near
impossible to see the world through anyone else's
eyes but our own.

… You were thinking of a purple penguin. See, told you I was a mind-reader!

SECRET IDENTITY

Her name is Jane. No, her name is Annabelle. Long blonde hair cascading down over narrow shoulders, she sits opposite and never once glances up from her romance novel. It is an escape for her. In a few short minutes she will be walking through the open-plan office and through to the kitchenette. Just as the coffee starts to drip into the pot she will feel a strong arm around her waist, making her jump. She spins around and he kisses her passionately.

Personal trainer Carl gets on just before the doors close and sits down. Placing his gym bag in between his legs, he pulls out his phone. Scrolling through text messages he grins as he stops at one. It is from his girlfriend Claire. No, it is from his boyfriend Brad. They are off to Vegas to get married and the flights have just been confirmed.

Music teacher Betty gets up, straightens her collar, and gets ready to leave. She looks tired. I am not surprised. Her newborn baby kept her up for most of the night.

As I walk towards the doors, Pilot Michael catches me in his periphery and looks up momentarily. I can't help but wonder who he sees standing next to him; Tom the photographer? James the lifeguard? Rufus the undercover police officer?

We all have a story, each one unique, and if we are lucky enough we get to see the real person behind the mask.

BLUE SPANDEX

There is that beautiful scene in Superman where our hero flies right up out of the Earth's atmosphere and using all his incredible strength and speed, circles our planet to reverse its spin. This turns back the clock and he is able to get to his beloved Lois just in time to save her life. She never finds out what her true love did for her on that sunny afternoon.

I have always been captivated by the power of love and what it can force us to do, whether we like it or not. It makes mothers lift up cars to save babies and people run into burning buildings to rescue a perfect stranger.

Heroes come in many shapes and sizes and even in the absence of blue lycra or a truth lasso, we are amazing. We can use our super-powered hearing to really listen to someone who desperately needs to be heard, and tune our X-ray vision to look right into the heart of someone who is hurting and needs a hug. Hell, we can even use our super strength to push through limitations and knock them right out of our way.

None of us are bulletproof, and at various points in our life we feel the impact of emotional shrapnel crashing into us, sometimes unexpectedly. Beneath the scars we are stronger and more heroic than we give ourselves credit for.

And sometimes the change from zero to hero can happen faster than you can run into a phone booth and spin around.

Now more than ever, this planet needs superheroes.

So what is your special power?

SEEING IN THE DARK

They say that if you are blind, all your other senses are heightened…

A good friend had taken us to a restaurant for the evening on a recent trip to Berlin. This was no ordinary eatery however, as I was soon to discover. We sat in the dimly lit bar and ordered a drink. After perusing the menu (being an indecisive person, it took me a while), I eventually settled on the four-course Vegetarian surprise.

Within a minute, I learnt that our waitress had long blonde hair, a smile to light up a room, and was almost completely blind. Placing my hands on Sandy's shoulders, we began our journey into the next room. Holding on for dear life she speedily led us through some heavy curtains into the pitch black restaurant. The sound of chattering diners and falling cutlery filled the room. Once comfortably seated she trundled off to bring us our first course...

And there we sat, speechless, in the dark. This was all too uncomfortable for words. The one thing I trusted to show me my place in the world was gone and I could no longer rely on my sight. Finally, after an internal battle, I decided to give in and swim in the darkness. My awareness expanded to fill the space and I felt more alive and alert than I had in a long time. Over the course of our meal we contemplated the meaning of love, life, and other amusements. It was beautiful.

Just as dessert was finally demolished, Sandy sat down next to us and we chatted for a while about what Berlin is like for her. I told her I would never look at my city with the same eyes again, and I imagined her smiling broadly as I led us out (do not even ask me how I did it, I have no idea).

Sometimes in life we find ourselves standing in darkness, unable to see what is truly around us. At times like this all we need to do is breathe, listen and wait for the answer.

Seeing is not always about using our eyes.

BROKEN EGGS

As the flour began to fall lightly through the sieve, I watched as the inside of the bowl turned white. Placing the sieve down, I reached for the first egg and sent it crashing down over the rim. A sudden crack filled the room as the contents splashed out into the dusty flour mound below. Soon the spotless work top became littered with shell shrapnel and I continued on, adding each ingredient until they were all together at last. I liked watching everything slowly come together with each stir of the spoon. It was like alchemy.

Once the final spoonful of mixture was dropped into its little paper case, I knew what was coming. I had no control over it and before I realised what was happening, my finger had made its way into the bowl, worked its way around the side and with a flourish, ended up in my mouth – my sweet reward.

Once they were in the safety of the oven, I had nothing to do but wait. As I surveyed the aftermath, I thought about the times in my life when things seemed so chaotic and messy. In the eye of the storm it seems like there is no light at the end of the tunnel and the knock-back is permanent - it never is however. Soon enough, if we're lucky, we can come out of the other side stronger and wiser with a much bigger heart.

In order to make a cake, we have to break a few eggs…but every difficult experience in life carries with it a gift. A gift of bringing us one step closer to the person we truly are inside.

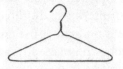

SECOND HAND

FOR SALE: A complete set of very well worn, second hand beliefs.

These have proven to be very useful to their previous owner and come in one size only.

You may find them a little restricting at times and they will almost certainly feel uncomfortable, causing imbalance and minor irritation. As the new owner you are obliged to carry them around 24/7 regardless of how heavy they are.

So what are you waiting for? Hurry as stocks won't last!

Everybody has an opinion about how the world works - "Nothing ever goes right, people can't be trusted, life is difficult…"

Sometimes we adopt these mantras as our own because we have heard them so many times in the past - surely they must be correct. And other times we don't even realise that they are subconsciously shaping the world around us in ways that may not necessarily be to our advantage.

These beliefs come from other people's experience of life and have nothing whatsoever to do with our own journey. The trick is to discover which ones limit our potential, keeping us earthbound and which ones inspire and lift, bringing us a step closer to flying. Once we are open to the idea of an internal spring clean, we can walk weightlessly down the high street until we eventually find the Prada Couture of beliefs about the world sparkling in the window, just waiting to be worn beautifully for the first time.

Go on, treat yourself...You are worth it!

STICKS AND STONES

I didn't see it coming at first. It arrived like a bolt out of the blue. The thing that first registered was the dull thud as the fist slammed into my face. Shockwaves suddenly rushed around my body like a fiery electrical storm. Adrenaline began to pump as I held back the tears. They would not get to see them today, they didn't deserve them. And so I fought them back harder than I had ever done before. Names continued to fly and echoed around the playground. Upon seeing our teacher striding towards us, the bullies fled and I suddenly found myself standing alone once again - saved by the dinner bell.

Growing up we are all told about sticks and stones, but the part about names never hurting us has never quite rung true. I, like most people on this planet, know that they can absolutely hurt...deeply.

Sometimes people can say wounding things.

Sometimes they sting momentarily, and others, the effects can last a lifetime.

But underneath everything, when someone throws

something hurtful our way, it is never really about us to begin with. They always reveal much more about the other person, and once we realise this, it makes it easier for us to forgive them and move on.

So when you think you're not special enough or good-looking enough or clever enough or thin enough, I am here to tell you that you are! You are perfectly amazing just the way you are!

RISKY BUSINESS

I saw it again last night whilst walking through the darkened alley towards home. In between finger-like branches, it shone out in the shadows like a harbinger of doom, taunting me, teasing me. Its message was clear and echoed loudly as I continued on my journey. The sign designed to strike fear into the heart of every man, woman and child, stared silently down from the external electric cupboard - 'Danger of Death' Averting my gaze, I looked up at the cloud-covered moon with thoughts of danger bouncing through my mind as I continued on.

We climb aboard rollercoasters, jump out of planes, swim with the sharks, and bungee off bridges. Aware of the hazards, we buckle up regardless and take that leap of faith into the unknown hoping that we will get to live happily ever after.

With everything in life, anything worth doing carries a risk. Whether it be leaving the house or falling in love, there is always a chance that someone will get hurt. But these are the things that make life sparkle.

Don't let the danger of death stop you from living - some things are worth the risk.

KEEPING UP WITH THE JONSES

Some people just have it all don't they! The immaculate home, the size 30 waist, the perfect job that you would do anything for. The smile on their face tells you that all is rosy in their manicured garden. You peep sneakily through the curtain to watch as the removal men take out each piece of furniture and make a mental note to start saving for that sofa in mocha and do 1000 more sit ups whilst waiting for it to arrive.

Surely then life will be flawless? After all, they seem to be extremely happy…

But are the Joneses trying frantically to keep up with the Patels, who are trying to keep up with the Smiths? We expend so much energy in life comparing ourselves to other people, we can momentarily forget who we really are. Instead of celebrating our beautiful uniqueness, we try to squeeze into a differently shaped hole which inevitably leads to us feeling not good enough.

The plain truth is that there is absolutely no one else

on this planet who can be you better than...well, you! We are the real deal, authentically perfect with all our imperfections.

WET WINGS

The first few drops of cool spring rain splash onto the dark pavement below and quickly cover the bustling city. I watch as the drops roll down the glass and leave behind a glistening, hypnotic trail.

Light from shop windows spill out to reflect off the wet pavement and bounce up into the twinkling night sky. Everything shimmers around the giant angel wings in the centre of the square. I love those wings, outstretched and ready to fly.

Rain falls harder now and forces people below to run for cover in doorways and seek refuge from the sudden downpour. I smile as I watch the weaving dance with a feeling of warmth washing over me. I am right where I'm meant to be.

A memory of getting soaked to the skin in Milan splashes into my mind and rolls back out again just as quickly.

There is that magnificent moment when your clothes get sodden and you feel the cool water begin to seep through onto warm skin. You realise that there is no point in running for cover. And so you stand in the moment and become part of the downpour. The surrender brings peace. Nothing else exists in that minute.

The rain begins to ease off and doorways are slowly becoming empty once again.

I should make my way outside now and down towards the tube...but not just yet. I want to watch the angel wings for a little while longer.

EXCESS BAGGAGE

I settle down onto the warm concrete ledge and wheel my bag closer in between my legs. As I lean forward to rest my arms upon it, a gust of wind whistles around the corner, up the steps, past the coffee shop and smashes into my face, forcing me to involuntarily close my eyes for a moment before continuing its journey towards the ticket hall and beyond. It is windy this afternoon despite the presence of blazing sun.

With my chin resting on my arms, I watch as people weave in and out of each other in a tangled dance of bodies and bags. It is fascinating.

And my mind begins to wander...I am catapulted back to the last time I stood in this station, surrounded by a sea of people and am instantly struck by associations.

As we navigate our way through life's twists and turns, inevitably, events can leave us with emotional baggage. Sometimes the weight is so minimal we barely notice it, and other times, it can feel like we are carrying around a big old house with absolutely no idea of how to get rid of it.

Every day holds a new lesson for us, and the challenge is to take the good from the bad and leave the rest behind.

And if we are lucky enough, we might just have people in our life who will help us unpack...

THE MAZE

Stepping inside, the sun vanishes from sight and the air around instantly cools my warm skin. And so I begin my journey to find the centre of the maze. Following the hedged wall around, I find myself facing the first choice of the afternoon: Left or right? I ponder this dilemma briefly before turning off to the left and continuing on through. There is something oddly comforting about being lost in here and I have no choice but to let go and listen to the birds sing knowingly all around.

Before long, once again, I am faced with another decision: Straight ahead or veer off to the right? Both pathways look tempting in an absolutely identical way. I turn off and continue on. I have been walking now for about twenty minutes, still none the wiser as to the location of my destination.

And as I journey onwards through the leafy maze, I begin to think about all the times I have felt lost. In life, there is no map to guide us. When we hit a wall, we have no choice but to stop, turn around and continue on a different path. Sometimes, we can put so much effort into something only to find ourselves right back where we started, we don't think we will ever have the energy to try again.

But regardless of whether we turn left or right, go straight ahead or turn back the way we came, there will always be another corner to take, another dead end to hit and another choice to make...and that's ok; we always find our way in the end.

And that afternoon I did, just when I least expected it.

TRACKS

As the train rocks gently from side to side, the monotonous sound of clickety-clack hypnotises me. I am caught in a trance. Gazing out across the horizon towards rolling fields and bushy hedgerows, I watch as the world whizzes by effortlessly. I am part of the blur.

Turning my head, I watch as the lovers opposite simultaneously take sips of hot coffee out of cardboard cups. The man to my right flips over his newspaper with a rustle, and laughter rings out a few seats in front; snapshots of people's journey imprinted in my mind forever.

Sleepily, I turn my attention back out of the window just in time to see a couple of Canada geese land gracefully onto the sparkling lake as we continue snaking onwards.

Life takes us in many different directions. Sometimes the journey is smooth and straight, other times, we are buffeted around in such a way that we can fall out of our seats. Some of the passengers on our train have been there from the very beginning, remaining for the entire journey as part of the furniture. Then there are the people who board for a few stops only. Their brief presence in our carriage infinitely enriches our life and changes us forever.

For a few moments nothing else exists. My eyes begin to close as I drift gently off into a deep sleep, trusting that I will awaken before my stop.

SIZE 8

My favourite shoes are a well-worn pair of red and white Converse All Star boots with matching double laces. I adore them. I wore them every day on tour in Italy and they have travelled with me thousands of miles like a trusted friend ever since. Sure, they are a bit battered, and the soles are slowly wearing down, but despite walking on pavement, grass, carpet, glass, gravel, sand, steel, and snow, they remain. Every inch of wear and tear seems to add a little more character than the day before. One of the bright red laces has shredded at the end following a vicious fight with an angry washing machine. They came out clean(ish) and still smiling at the memory of having once strolled along the Seine at dusk.

We take so many steps in this lifetime that it would be impossible to keep count. Sometimes they are so small, they hardly make an imprint, steadily ambling along. And occasionally the strides are so colossal that we literally vault into a new chapter without so much as a glance behind.

Everyone wears their shoes differently and each pair has their own unique story to tell. Despite all the weight they carry on their journey, they never give up, steady in the knowledge that no one will ever be able to walk a mile in them better than their rightful owner.

THERE'S SOMETHING ABOUT HELEN

As she held out her hand I noticed her perfectly polished nails which shone a deep red in the dimly lit cabaret bar. Her long brown hair glistened as she popped up onto a stool next to me and settled in at the bar. Drink in hand, we wished our mutual friend 'break a leg', as he turned and walked backstage to get ready for the show.

There was a shy confidence about her and I liked the way that her eyes would glance briefly at the floor before answering a question.

We talked about theatre, music and travel. I laughed a lot. She was charming and intelligent.

Stepping onto the last tube train of the evening, I followed her to take a seat and watched as the doors closed.

As we set off I began to notice that other people were interested in Helen too. Her lightness filled the carriage and the passengers could not help but look in her direction. There was a buzz in the air that I hadn't noticed before, and so, we continued chatting until the train slowed to signal my stop. Slinging my bag across my body, I wished her goodbye and said how much I had enjoyed her company. I kissed her cheek, gave her a hug, and stepped out onto the warm, empty platform.

Watching the bright lights of the train slowly accelerate and vanish into the dark tunnel once more, I suddenly felt moved.

Once out into the cool night air, I found myself wondering at what point she had realised that she was living in the wrong body.

Her personal courage and conviction was stunning, and despite now being a woman, her balls were bigger than any I had seen before.

Fear often stops us from declaring to the world who we truly are, and the more honest we are with ourselves and others, the more inspiring and beautiful we become.

THE CANYON

I fastened my seat belt tightly, checked it, and tugged on it again for good measure. I pulled on my headphones as the propellers began to turn, quickly matching the speed of my thoughts. In a few short seconds, with all the pre-flight checks made, the tarmac gently drifted away from us as we took to the air. I couldn't believe that I was actually doing the one thing which I vowed I would never do.
In that moment, I realised I had no choice but to let go of everything. From way up here, the only thing I had any control over were my thoughts. I decided that I wouldn't miss this for the world - and so I breathed deeply. With every intake of air, I felt my body relax and let go. I suddenly began to smile as I looked down over the Hoover Dam, the sun glistening on the water. Circling around, we continued up and out towards the canyon.
After gently touching down onto rocky earth, I stepped out into one of the seven natural wonders of the world. I looked out across the horizon and

couldn't help but wonder about the nature of fear and how it can prevent us from doing certain things in life; moments that enrich and colour the world around us.

Sometimes in life, we have to embrace our fears and do the one thing that terrifies us the most in order to feel truly alive.

And in that moment, I felt more alive than ever before.

STRIKE

The ball rolls up the ramp and gently clunks into the one in front. My favourite is still the glittery blue one that reminds me of a moonlit swimming pool... but that was too heavy. Shame. It totally went with my outfit. Then there was the mauve ball...too light. Eventually I had settled on the matt green one that was just right. I wondered if Goldilocks would have had this much trouble choosing.

I slide my fingers into the holes and take a step forward for the penultimate time. Swinging the ball, it lurches forward as I release my grip, and watch as it hits the floor with a dull thud. Suddenly picking up momentum, it rolls quickly down the alley and smashes slightly off-centre. All but two pins remain; and there they stand, taunting me in the distance...

I wait impatiently for my trusty ball to come rolling back as I visualise the pins falling to the ground, followed by rapturous applause and fireworks. Second place was within my grasp.

A flutter of excitement grows in my tummy as I send

the ball flying towards its final destination. It is veering dangerously to the left...it will correct itself in a minute...any minute now...and so I believe right up until the moment it plops into the gutter.

Shrugging my shoulders, I turn, laugh, and make my way back to a cold beer.

Sometimes in life, things don't turn out the way we would like them to. As much as we want it, we don't always get that job, that person doesn't always love us back and our lottery numbers never seem to come up; but that's life. Everything happens for a reason and maybe, something even more amazing is waiting just around the corner.

DINOSAURS AND ICE

As I say goodbye to the Diplodocus, I move smoothly through the revolving glass door and come out into the cold December evening. Walking down the steps, I turn my head to gaze down the length of this cathedral-like building and am immediately thrown back to when I first came to the museum as a child. It was like a dream, magical. Decades later, I am still awestruck by its sheer magnificence. Sparkling trees line the path, encompassing everyone in a festive cocoon and fills me with a sense of warmth and cosiness.

As I reach the ice rink bathed in blue light, something makes me want to stop. I stand there leaning against the thick Perspex wall and rest my head on folded arms. I watch as people wrapped up in woolly hats and scarves weave in and out of each other, circling, gliding. A smile creeps across my face as a couple struggles to stay upright on the ice. Like newborn lambs with limbs moving in all directions, they eventually land entwined onto the cold ice and I can't help but join in with their infectious loud laughter. Then as the wind begins to pick up, I find myself drift off into thought. Our journey through life is rarely smooth. There are days when we glide effortlessly along the ice, picking up speed and dancing as we go. Then there are moments where we just can't find our balance. Despite all our best efforts we still land flat on our face...but that's ok.

Nothing is for nothing, and sometimes it takes a fall to get us back on track. The best we can do is put both hands on the ground, push ourselves up and straighten our hair once again...For we are much stronger than we know.

THE LIGHTNESS OF LOVE

The thing that first attracted me to it was the way in which the wings would slowly open and close to reveal bright blue eye-like markings that shimmered in the sunlight. With each gust of breeze, its legs would stiffen to resist being removed involuntarily from the summer-scented lilac upon which it rested. I had never seen anything so incredible in all my nine years of life.

Steadily holding the jar with tiny hands, I placed it over the butterfly and snapped the lid closed, trapping the clump of lilac inside with it.

Once indoors, I decided to let it fly free. There was something extremely surreal about watching it flutter around my bedroom and then come to rest on the blue curtains. I loved the feel of the silky wings in my hands and how the iridescent powder would rub off onto my fingers, making them shimmer a little.

Something was wrong…

I quickly realised that bit by bit, the colour was fading from its delicate wings the more I held it, and instead of the usual circling and soaring above my head, it would now flutter clumsily to the floor.

I knew I had to let it go. Placing it gently back into the palm of my hand, I carried it downstairs and out onto the branch from whence it came. I watched it for a while until it was time to go in for dinner and said my goodbye.

Sometimes we try so hard to hold onto the things we love for fear of losing them, it is exhausting. Love lands where it is meant to, and just like a beautiful butterfly, will come to rest gently in your hand when the time is right.

I DO

Stepping out of the cool dark church, the sun kissed my face through the trees, momentarily blinding me. Then as my vision cleared, I saw her...
Leaning in the doorway, I watched as all those around made last minute adjustments, and was transfixed at the way the gentle gust of wind played and danced around the fluttering train. Hairs on my arms stood up as my eyes ever so slightly misted. There was magic around that morning, and for the briefest of moments everything stopped still.
I thought about her prince who waited patiently inside for her arrival and had no idea what was happening just outside the stone walls.
Smiling, I put my hand to my lips, blew her a kiss and turned to take my seat inside. Then a thought occurred to me: the love that was pulled into existence decades ago, as her beautiful mum stepped through that same doorway on a chilly February morning to meet her own prince, remained. Love had come around full circle - it stood stoically through

52

snow, rain, and blistering heat.
And it waited and waited for this very day, undiluted
by the years which have washed over it.
Every single piece of love we pull from our hearts will
always remain, shining brightly for all to see.

ROOM 209

The keycard goes in, the light turns green, and I swing open the door.

Falling back onto the bed, crisp white linen crumples around me as I lie there in the darkness. There's no urgency to illuminate my surroundings, not yet. I remain there frozen in time. For now, this is right where I'm meant to be.

It's funny how wherever one goes in the world, hotel rooms all have the same ambience, the familiar in an unfamiliar city. Memories of a year living out of them come back in an instant. I relive every minute in glorious Technicolor as if watching a montage in a movie, accompanied by instrumental music. Laughter and tears resonate through my mind as they carry me across an ocean.

The sound of a door opening and closing somewhere down the corridor pulls me abruptly from my reverie just as the air conditioning unit clicks on and whirs into action.

Thoughts turn to the other guests above and below

who are settling down for the evening in their rooms. I wonder what they are doing right now; watching trashy TV? Saying goodnight to a child on the phone? Brushing their teeth whilst thinking about their meeting tomorrow? The endless possibilities contained within the hotel grounds suddenly make the world seem a bigger place.

I roll over and reach into the darkness. Finding the button, I wake up my phone: 23:42. In a moment, I will turn on my bedside lamp and get ready for bed, but not yet. I want to swim in this room for a little while longer.

59 SECONDS

59 seconds...

My arms fling around her neck and I pull her in tightly. There we stand in our embrace. The world stops spinning as I feel her chest move in and out with every breath. I can smell her perfume. It throws me right back. With all my might, I pull away and look into her smiling face. Her auburn hair glistens in the sun and blows ever so gently in the breeze.

47 seconds...

I am finding it hard to form words but I know that I don't have long.

"I have so many questions to ask, I don't know where to begin. Where have you been all this time? I couldn't find you anywhere".

She smiles.

"I didn't go anywhere, my darling. I have been here with you the whole time. Remember the day you stood looking over at the ocean and tears ran down your face? I was there holding you. Just look in the mirror; you have my eyes".

30 seconds...

"Do you have any regrets?"

She thinks about this question for a second.

"Life is too short for regrets. Every choice we make takes us to another place. There is no right or wrong; just life experience. We always get to where we are meant to be eventually anyway. Trust your instincts".

18 seconds...

A breeze picks up and swirls pink blossom around us.

"Why does life sometimes feel so hard? Some days it feels impossible to move through".

Her hands lift up towards my face and as they hold onto me, she looks directly into my eyes.

"There will always be challenges to overcome. That is part of life. Please remember, these are only opportunities to show the world who you really are. We are stronger than our bodies give us credit for. Use these times to shine, my darling".

7 seconds...

A wave of anger washes over me as I realise that this is it.

"I miss you so much. I wish you were always here. I have so many questions still to ask".

"I know my angel, I know. Everything we need to know is inside each and every one of us. Never forget how much I love you. I live in your heart. You are never alone".

1 second...

I hug her so tightly; I worry that she might break. The wind picks up...and she is gone. Just one more minute...

THE MISSING GIFT

I have looked under the sofa and in the bed, around the TV and above the wardrobe... Still it eludes me like an invisible city fox. The worst thing about it is, I have only just realised how precious it was - In the early hours of Sunday morning, 60 minutes went missing!

The absence of this lost hour leaves me with a pocketful of questions and a silver lining of sunny mornings and balmy nights ahead.

Time has a clever way of slipping by unnoticed if we turn our heads for too long. The truly amazing things we can do in those 3,600 seconds are mind-blowing. Everything can change in that moment. You can say 'I love you!', 'Never again!' and 'I do!'

Possibilities fill every single minute, and if we could just realise how fleeting time is, we would never waste any of it again, not a tiny drop.

Just think how rich life would be for us all if we let go of the past and future and lived for the now. That is where our power truly lies.

As with most things in life, nothing is ever really lost, and I feel a warmth inside to know that this absent hour is going to fly back to me in a few months' time, carrying a gift of a second chance to make a difference.

SEASONS OF CHANGE

It happens once a year and every time it creeps up so silently, it takes a while to realise that things have actually changed.

Usually, it comes with a slight drop in temperature, then a subtle adjustment in the quality of light. Mornings grow slightly darker and evening sunsets show up just that little bit earlier.

Walking towards the cocoon of the tube, I look down, and there they were - adorning the pavement with gold, amber, and russet: leaves that were once a bright green now lay crisping at my feet. Where did they come from? I don't remember seeing them yesterday. Something magical happened overnight. The season changed and brought with it new opportunities to let go and move forward. For a while it looked as if everything was dying. Trees grow bare and a chill hits the air.

It is a perfect time to reflect on the year and glance at the things that have happened over the passing months. Autumn is a season for stripping everything away and gently releasing old habits to start afresh, safe in the knowledge that every season is just a new beginning. It is refreshing to take a moment to feel the shift happening all around us and become a part of it.

I take that moment now as I playfully kick the leaves and watch as they displace and settle. A sense of freedom washes over me as I fasten my coat up against the cool evening air, and continue the journey home.

CHATTER

Ooh, it is nice and warm in here - I wonder if the heating is on or if the chef has the oven door open...this is a good table - I like window seats...I wonder how my hair looks after being caught in the wind..."Hi, just a beer please, my friend will be turning up in a minute"...It is quiet in here tonight...nice candle - would be lovely with a bubble bath...everyone here is in a couple...I wonder if they think I am eating alone…maybe people are whispering that I don't have any friends - that would be embarrassing...The wax on my finger is starting to burn a little - just leave the candle alone...If I get my phone out, they will think that I am busy and have lots to do - no new messages...I hope she turns up soon, I feel like people are looking over...Another swig of beer I think - it's nearly finished already...I remember this song from years ago...Mmm what do I fancy to eat?
We try every trick in the book to distract ourselves. We read, text, hum, think, ponder, remember and

wish. It occurs to me as I sit here waiting, that the one thing we very rarely do is just be; to still the mind and free ourselves from all the chatter that acts as a constant narrator to life. I can't help but wonder what lies in the silence - the secret to life, eternal youth, this week's lottery numbers?

I make a quick mental note to investigate this further before the door swings open and I hear the muffled words from behind "I am meeting a friend, he's over there by the window". I smile, welcoming the interruption.

CONCRETE COMPANION

I move through the veins of the city with the greatest of ease. The streets know all my secrets - they have been there from the very beginning. Supportive of weighty thoughts and lofty dreams, they hold me high and carry me along.

Each brand new pair of shoes I sport are met with a cheeky grin.

There has always been something comforting about getting lost in a city. Each unexplored side road brings a new adventure and fresh hope.

As the busy streets begin to envelop every part of me, I can't help but realise that the next time I stride along this pavement, I will be a different person, a new version of myself. Life will have taken me further on my journey and changed me forever.

I feel the first few drops of winter rain hit the top of my head and suddenly notice that the pavement is already altering with every splash of water crashing onto its cold, grey surface. And I walk. I have been walking these streets for over a decade and know every intimate detail. They remember me; they have

been there for me, stoically supportive with every step. They have witnessed the laughter and tears, the hopes and fears, never once leaving my side.
The streets of the city run through my heart and carry with them all of my dreams. Like a trusty old friend they remain, and patiently look forward to the day they will see me again.

THE FEAR

I place my fingers through the flowing water and wait until the temperature is just right. Stepping into the bath, the cold hits the soles of my feet as I pull the curtain closed. My body is soaked in seconds and I sigh with contentment as warm water runs down over my face….

Suddenly I am stopped dead in my tracks with shampoo still covering my hair. Where did that bang come from? Instinct tells me to open my eyes and see what made the noise but the soap now running over my face stops me from doing so. I stand there with eyes tightly closed listening to the sound of water splashing into the bath and escaping down the plughole.

At that moment a million images flash through my mind at breakneck speed. I see a man wearing a balaclava, rifling through my underwear drawer, and I see a framed photograph being projected across the room by an angry spirit, and I see the shower scene in Psycho being played out in glorious Technicolor;

previews of what awaits me just beyond the dripping curtain.

Quickly rinsing the soap from my eyes, I turn off the water and jump out onto the bath mat. I fling a towel around my waist (one has to retain some semblance of dignity, even when facing ghoulish monsters) and step off the mat. Courage built up, I stride into the bedroom to find...nothing! Everything is just as I left it except for the wet footprints which now mark the room.

That's the funny thing about fear. We can build situations up so much in our minds that they sometimes appear bigger than they actually are. In reality nothing is more terrifying than the fear itself and once we turn to face it head on, we wonder what we were so scared of in the first place.

A PIECE OF PEACE

Sunday morning in the city. Even at 6.30am, there is a buzz in the air. As I sneak a peek from behind the blinds, there is something about the morning light that piques my interest. I have been awake for a while now and, resigned to the fact that I'm not getting back to sleep any time soon, I get up and turn on the coffee machine.

There has been so much rain lately; this blue, cloudless sky brings hope of a lovely day. The ghostly moon, still visible, is obscured momentarily by a plane's contrails cutting across its surface. Picking up my favourite mug, I take a sip of hot, freshly brewed coffee.

A dog barks in the distance. I wonder what he has seen to make him so vocal at this time of the morning.

Sitting here on the balcony, I am amazed at how much is going on right now. The constant hum of traffic resonates all around me, framed only by singing birds and honking geese.

Right now, I'm happy, able to breathe for the first

time in ages.

A memory of waking up in an Italian hotel somewhere flashes through my mind and vanishes just as quickly, leaving behind the echo of a forgotten feeling.

I watch as a pair of Canada geese sweep gracefully overhead and notice for the first time this morning that the sun is reflecting off the canal, sending its shimmering light through the trees.

Right now, in my contentedness, I feel connected to everything that is around me, and as I finish off the last of my coffee, I make a promise to come to this place again soon.

LUNCHTIME IN PARIS

Weaving in and out of the lunchtime traffic, streets come and go in a Parisian haze. The last of the summer sun shines brightly through the window and bathes my face in light. I feel my tummy rumble deeply and all I can think about is the wonderful meal that lies ahead. The reviews called the restaurant 'A delightful treasure trove' and I couldn't wait.

Paying the taxi driver, we step out onto the warm cobbled street and watch as the car vanishes around the corner.

The first thing that strikes me as odd is the absence of light in the building...then the absence of custom. When I finally realise that there is also an absence of restaurant inside, I know that it is game over.

With a promise of 'The best food in the whole of Paris', it was onto plan B. Our spirits lift as we hail a passing taxi and, once again, streets come and go in a Parisian haze; the sun still shining brightly, stomach still rumbling like thunder.

" Désolé, nous sommes fermés pour les entreprises!"

announces the sign, taped loosely to the door. Even with limited knowledge of the French language, I knew this wasn't good. Turning helplessly we watch the taxi speed off into the distance. We look at each other blankly. If I wasn't so hungry, I would have laughed.

And so we give up on our search for the 'Best places to eat in Paris'. We're too tired to care anymore. Not expecting an answer, we ask a little old man where we could eat. He smiles, leans on his broom, and points our way to a 'Sweet little bar with a lovely atmosphere' just down a narrow side alley. These reviews were getting more unbelievable by the minute and so, skeptically, we turn the corner to find a simple establishment half way down, furnished in dark wood, dim lighting and adorned with a scruffy grey dog sitting in the doorway. Stepping carefully over him, a bohemian looking woman greets us and ushers us inside.

"We have stopped serving food, I'm sorry", says our waitress as she pulls a sad face and brushes the hair out of her eyes to tuck it behind ear. Our hearts sink. "I can bring you some cheese, wine and crusty bread instead if you like?"

We smile broadly as it arrives at the table; a veritable feast lay before us. And so we sit there all afternoon without a care in the world, laughing and talking about life. A wave of happiness washes over me as I realise, right at this moment, I was exactly where I was meant to be.

BROKEN WINGS

I always made sure that I got to my spot just in time
to watch the sun disappear over the horizon and into
the sea. Sitting on cool pebbles, I waited for the
spectacle to begin with just the sound of lapping
waves and squawking gulls to keep me company.
I knew when it was about to start by the eerie silence
that washed over the abandoned pier. I would wait
and wait and wait...
Then all at once, they appeared; hundreds of starlings
would burst out into the crimson sky and begin to
swarm around like bees, weaving in and out of each
other as if choreographed by Matthew Bourne
himself. Transfixed by their aerial acrobatics, every
twist and turn took my breath away. It was a beautiful
show worthy of a standing ovation.
Our own style of flight changes from day to day;
Sometimes we glide effortlessly like an eagle, wings
spread, riding high on warm currents and a gentle
breeze. Other days, like a swallow, we flap manically
just to stay aloft through life's challenges and our
wings are left a little battered and bruised. These are

the moments in which we think we will never fly
again...
But we always do. We were designed that way.

THE FOG

As I sleepily pulled open the blinds, something was different. It took me a few seconds to realise that everything had vanished. Mother Nature had pulled off one of her greatest illusions whilst I was asleep. All 800ft of glass, steel and concrete was gone in a theatrical flourish. Even the flashing beacon at the apex had disappeared. Canary Wharf had vanished along with everything else around it. David Copperfield couldn't have done it better.

Zipping up my jacket, I took my first step outside just as the damp scent hit my nostrils and rushed down into my lungs. An eerie blanket of dense fog replaced the horizon with nothing but silhouettes of bare trees to guide the way. The world seemed like a different place.

Journeying into the thick of it I couldn't help but wonder what it is to feel lost. Sometimes we find ourselves in a personal fog with no sense of direction and our questions are met with silence. The sense of disorientation is palpable; we forget that beyond the clouds is a bright shining sun of potential that has been present the whole time.

Some days are more dazzling than others, and sometimes we just need to get caught in a fog in order to see things clearly.

LOOSE STRINGS

As soon as it happened I knew there was something horribly wrong! I had carefully place three fingers one by one on their strings and, finding their home, held them firmly in place to listen as the other hand stroked gently downwards. A discordant noise rang out of the room and floated off into the hallway, making a cat somewhere in the distance run off and hide quivering under a bush. Surely it shouldn't need tuning again? I only did it a couple of weeks ago and haven't played it since...Hmmm, ok, maybe it did. There is something quite therapeutic about tuning my guitar. The combination of listening closely to the vibration until it feels right is fascinating. It is always painfully difficult to ignore when a musical instrument needs tuning, and as I begin to tighten the strings, I can't help but wonder why it isn't as obvious when our lives are just as out of tune - suddenly our hearing isn't as acute.

Sometimes we forget to look at our lives and attitudes regularly, and without realising it, some of our beliefs can quickly go out of harmony with who we truly are. People around us can have such an effect on us that our strings change. Every day we shift ever so slightly, and we need to give ourselves a regular emotional tune up so we are the most authentic version of ourselves possible.

It's important to take that moment to listen to your life and pay close attention to the notes being played; What kind of symphony is being created, and is it the best melody for you?

NEVER MIND THE GAP

As I pull my favourite blue Japanese cotton scarf up around my ears, I make my way down the steps and onto the empty platform. For some reason there doesn't seem to be a soul around this evening. I walk up to the pillar that holds up the roof, and lean against it. For a brief moment I am lost in the music flowing through my earphones and straight into my heart. There has been a chill in the air of late and for the first time this season, I watch as warm breath leaves my body and disappears into the cool wintry night.

And so I lean with hands in pockets, looking down along the silvery tracks that snake off miles into the distance.

Then something pulls my focus.

I glance down and notice three words printed boldly onto the cold concrete. How had I missed them until now?

MIND THE GAP.

These ten little letters suddenly get my mind spiraling

off as I begin to think about the gaps in our lives - the space we have to cross to get to where we want to be. We tell ourselves 'I will be happy once I've lost the weight, and got that job, fallen in love, and made that money'. And when we eventually do get these things, we barely notice their presence in our lives because we are too busy thinking about how we won't be content until we get that car and go on that holiday, have that baby, and get the promotion.

I can't help but wonder if we are always in the gap. That space in between where we have just come from and where we are going. Maybe that's all there is anyway.

And could it be that within this gap lies our true potential? The potential to be courageous, loving, forgiving, inspiring, creative, generous, sparkling and fabulous?

RIPPLES

There is a time of day that sits just before the sun comes up and the city is still rubbing its eyes, that I dedicate to me, just to me and no one else. I love feeling the cool water rush over my body as I submerge my entire being, and for the briefest of moments, vanish from sight like a Vegas illusionist. Everything becomes a muffled echo as I sink deeper into this chlorine-scented world. Here under the surface, everything feels safe as I am quickly emancipated from the demands and deadlines that hover just above the surface. Despite not having any air down here, I can once again breathe deeply. Limbs moving in harmony to travel a length at a time. The rhythm inducing an almost out of body experience, allowing my mind to venture outside of its natural habitat and explore the boundaries of thought to come up with new, inventive ways of being. I am free and happy.

Life seems to be so full nowadays and it feels as if we never have enough time to do everything. Stress has become the new normal and tiredness is the new status symbol. So many things demand our attention and the fear of not having ample time to reach our full potential is palpable. It is so important to have our moment in the day where we can push the panic button on life and just swim in the stillness. Here we can truly listen to the inner voice - the voice that guides us and knows what is important. The voice that knows we are always going to be ok.

TEA FOR TWO

"What would you like to drink?"

"Hmmmm, do you have any herbal tea?"

My host's knowing chuckle echoed loudly in my ears as the cupboard door swung open with a flourish. I half expected to discover a bikini-clad assistant inside waiting to vanish in a puff of theatrical smoke.

Instead, the most colourful array of teas and coffees never before seen outside a supermarket lay before me.

"I don't even like half of these, but I love to be able to offer my guests anything they like; I want them to be happy", he said pulling a face. I laughed.

Slowly sipping on my newly opened Lemon and Ginger tea I couldn't help but think about what this meant. Instantly I felt special.

It was such a small thing really but the warmth and thoughtfulness of it made me smile.

I wondered about how many other people had sat at

this kitchen table and sipped on a cup of carefully chosen Chamomile, Darjeeling, or Rosehip & Elderflower...

We all love it when someone does something to make us feel special and unique - that warm glow inside as a sense of happiness washes over us.

Every day there are opportunities all around in which we can make someone feel just that little bit better - whether it be with a genuine smile, a touch or just holding a door open.

Taking the time to acknowledge a friend or colleague's nice new haircut can make their day and send a ripple out into the world.

Some people say that it's the small things that matter the most, and as I drink the last drops of my tea, I know this to be true.

LOVELY EXTRAVAGANCE

There I was, 8 years old with my amazing A-Team duvet cover pulled up over my head, a question burning into my brain. It was keeping me awake and I needed an answer: How many people in the world can you love at any one time, and does the heart eventually fill up like my shoebox crammed full of Transformers? I drifted off to sleep that night having used up all of the fingers on both my tiny hands to count with, still no closer to a solution.

27 years and several loves later I am realising something: with all the things that should be used sparingly in life, love isn't one of them.

So I say let's be extravagant! Never be afraid to shout it, sing it, whisper it, scream it, chant it, show it, feel it or write it. Exercise no caution. Let it all fly out! It's surprising how the more we give, the more we have to give.

Opportunities to express love in all its forms are everywhere. We need to take our love ration books, tear them into a million pieces, and throw them up into the air to watch as the pieces of our heart flutter outwards and land wherever they are needed.

THE NAUGHTY STEP

Right, that's it! Go and sit on the naughty step and have a long, hard think about what you've done!

Okay, so while we are sitting here for a bit, I wanted to ask you something. Have you been here before? I have, many times! Not for refusing to eat my greens or for being cheeky or even for not tidying my room (the floordrobe I have is a walk-in by the way). The step I am talking about is the place we go to voluntarily punish ourselves. The space in which the internal monologue throws all the shoulda-woulda-coulda's in our face and tells us how stupid we were. We mull it over until our head hurts. All of that self-flagellation leaving deep red marks in our minds and conscience.

So when will we give ourselves permission to get up off the step and forgive ourselves; crime and time done, finito?

It seems that out of habit, the naughty step has

become our home from home; like a self-imposed prison of guilt that we have furnished to make the whole beating-ourselves-up experience more comfortable.

We miss so much by looking back at the things we may have said or done. If we can't make things right then it's time to draw a line under it, move on and vow never to do that again and congratulate ourselves on being one step closer to becoming a better person with a more open heart.

SHINY AND NEW

There they were - a thing of beauty and shining like a beacon of hope in this scary, new city. I knew I wanted them as soon as I saw them. I had saved up some money by skillfully reducing that week's menu down to a jar of sandwich spread and salted crackers - Delia would have been impressed (or horrified). I watched as the sales assistant popped them into the blue plastic bag and bade my new best friend and I farewell.

A rush of pure excitement flooded through me as I sat on the end of the bed and began pulling them up over each leg.

That night we danced like never before. No one else existed; it was just us against the music. We were indestructible.

The sun was already coming up by the time I walked out into the dawn. Snaking my way through the veins of the city I watched as the streets started to slowly wake and rub its eyes.

I had completely forgotten about my silver trousers

by the time I arrived home.

It took me a couple of seconds to notice the singer/songwriter Cathy Dennis standing there with an entourage of charity workers, blocking the way. After saying good morning, they cheerfully explained that their charity needed an extra person to pose for a promotional picture. As I was there (and sporting the brightest legs in Soho) I reluctantly agreed, suddenly feeling slightly overdressed for the occasion. Smiling broadly, I watched as the photographer began clicking the camera, marking the beginning of this wonderfully strange day.

Several makeovers later I can't help but chuckle. No matter where we go in life or whoever we meet along our journey, there will always be 'moments' that take our breath away. Some will be amazing and some challenging, but they all make us who we are today and if we are lucky, we get to wear silver trousers along the way.

BIRTHDAY

It's her birthday. She is only 4 years old but I feel as if she's been around our entire life. The room is filled with elegantly wrapped presents and everyone within the four walls, consumed by lightness. Occasional squeals of delight fly out as presents are opened and instantly loved.

With a flick of her hair she pushes a fallen sleeve back up and reaches down to open another card. Turning it over, her face illuminates the entire world as she holds it aloft as if it were a gold medal.

'I got a heart!', she laughs excitedly showing off the sketch on the back of the bright red envelope.

A wave of love washes over me and forces a lump up into my throat. She is an angel.

And so we all look on at the girl who is giving us hope of dreams coming true and sunnier days ahead. Candles are lit, lights turn off and singing begins. Bathed in the flickering glow I can't help but think about the last time we sang this song and how much has happened in the space in between.

We never quite know where a year will take us. We

celebrate the triumphs, we mourn the losses. We sing, we dance, we cry and we change. It is more than just seasons and months, days and minutes - it is about the moments and what we chose to do within them. We dare to dream in spite of fear, sometimes succeeding, sometimes not.

And occasionally if we're really lucky, nowhere will lead to somewhere - that place where we realise that we might just be more incredible than we ever thought possible.

MOMENTS

Autumnal evening rain begins to fall. The sky was blue when I left the house this morning, and now cool drops are finding their way onto my face as strangers around me begin to rush home.

I make my way up the steps towards the platform and look up at the illuminated board.

Next train: 4 minutes.

At least I'm undercover. And so I stand there at the top, sheltered from the rain, looking around.

I watch as a couple on the other platform walk slowly from one end to the other pulling heavy cases behind them. I wonder where they have travelled from and where they are going. The only other person on the platform is a man sitting at the end, engrossed in the evening edition of a newspaper. I wonder what story he is reading and what he makes of this crazy, beautiful world we live in. My attention is pulled upwards as a plane begins to climb noisily away from City Airport. Soon it will be high above the clouds just in time to catch the last glimpse of a burning

sunset invisible to the rest of us down here.
Next train: 2 minutes.
My mind starts to wander and I think about how everything seems to be in a constant state of change. Conversations and moments flood my mind as rain continues to fall onto glistening concrete.
And then I realise something.
I will never again be standing on this platform, watching these particular people on this wet, late September evening. As soon as I leave here, this moment will be gone...forever.
As the train pulls gently in, I'm reminded that wherever we go in life and whatever we do, we only ever have this moment...
And everything's perfect!

ABOUT THE AUTHOR

Jeff is a trained actor working for over a decade in theatre, TV and film. After returning from a 6-month tour in the musical 'Jekyll & Hyde', he started his weekly blog (www.malleablereality.com) that takes the reader on a journey through the everyday/ordinary to discover the life lessons hidden in every situation. He also has a regular column in magazines such as 'Healing Connections' and 'PoV'.

ABOUT THE ILLUSTRATOR

Sean studied Fine Art at Central Saint Martins, and is now a freelance illustrator/artist taking commissions from around the world.

If you would like to get in touch with Jeff about this book, or would like some further information on Sean, email him at jeffchandler00@aol.com

Love and Light!

Printed in Great Britain
by Amazon.co.uk, Ltd.,
Marston Gate.